Sidonia's Chronicles:
My Story of Courage, Because I am Ready to Come Out!

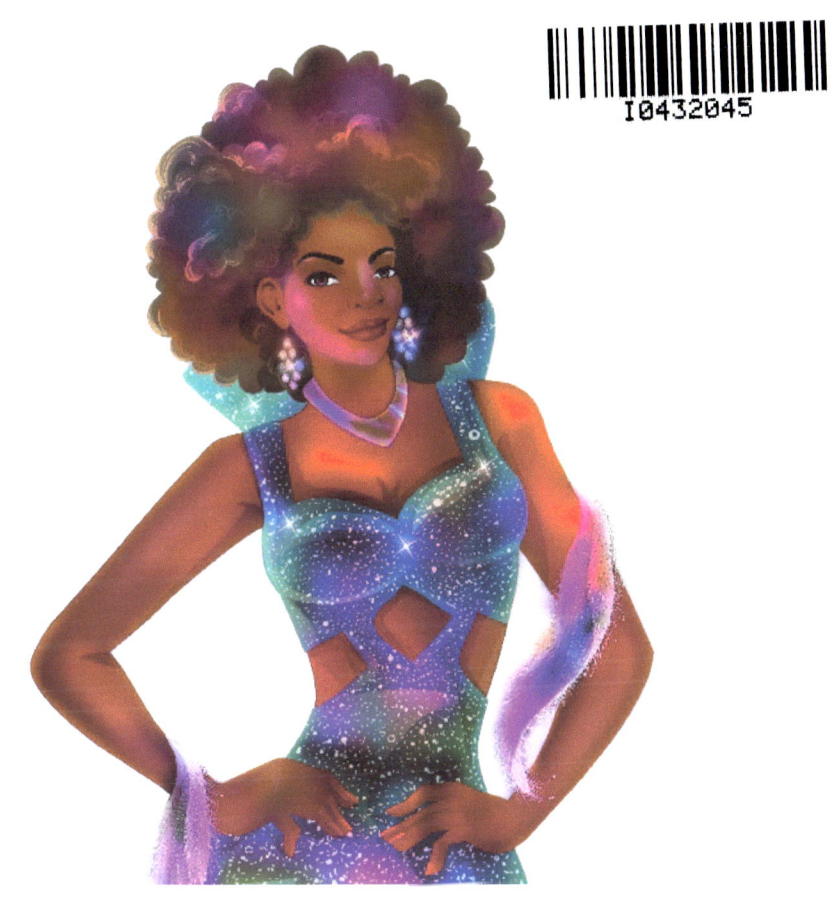

DR. ALLANA E. TODMAN DA GRACA

Sidonia's Chronicles: My Story of Courage, Because I am Ready to Come Out!

Sidonia's Chronicles:
My Story of Courage, Because I am Ready to Come Out!

Dr. Allana Da Graca

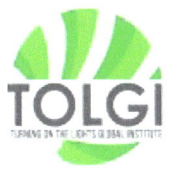

Sidonia's Chronicles:
My Story of Courage, Because I am Ready to Come Out!

Copyright © 2020 Dr. Allana Da Graca

All rights reserved. No part of this book may be used or reproduced by any means, graphics, electronic, or mechanical, including photocopying, recording copying, taping, or by any information storage retrieval system without the written permission of the publisher except in the case of brief quotations embodied in critical articles and reviews.

TOLGI publishing may be contacted by contacting
Turning On the Lights Global Institute
177 Huntington Ave
Suite 1700
Boston Ma, 02115

Sidonia's Chronicles

Sidonia's Exposition	9
Confessions	13
I Need A Life Jacket	15
Anger pangs	17
This path	18
Solace	20
Reflections	21
Face to Face	22
Now	24
Sidonia: 120 Days Choreopoem	26
You are beautiful	30
The Fourth Wind	32
This is my day	35
My Uncle Turtle	36
Ms. Polly redemption	39
#Stayhome	44
Empty Trees	46
Leaving	48
Fly Like An Eagle	49

Unveiling ME	51
Empowerment	54
Uncle turtle Part 2	55
Stories of Courage	58

Sidonia's Exposition

I wish I never had to write this story, but if I don't tell it

`It may die with me.

Lord knows too much has happened

For me to take another dream to the Grave

In my memory, I am brought to a hand that tugs at my shirt

Ms. Polly---second cousin on my father's side--

Stepped in after my mother died

at the thought of another stare down from Capital H in ER.

My throat constricts

and I feel like I'm going to pass out,

but that only happens to old people.

I just make this **Shame** turn in my stomach

it almost feels like I have the runs

I am lactose

 like I had many glasses of chocolate milk

but still, the release won't relent

When you look at

me

you see an empty canvas

and base your questions

 on outside perceptions

but

I want to know if you care

Layers beneath my scars

little Sidonia

A chocolate girl with a big afro

Ms. Polly said:

"It's ok if you are a **tar baby**, at least you can find a job if you get your high school diploma."

To me, **Ms. Polly was GOD**;

I trusted her words

I would return to my room desperately and pray:

"Lord, did you intentionally make me ugly? Did you intentionally leave me in the care of someone who really only sees me as a burden? I wish with all of my heart to be somewhere different."

Ms. Polly stares at Me.

She was a fair-skinned lady and would comment that she did not like my melanin. She liked it, but felt it **offended her potential** when we went to important events.

I hated her Stares

Her stares told me that I was not **worthy of love** ……………

She taught me a number of lessons:

Number one

always say yes

Number two

never ever share your real thoughts

Number three

Always praise HER

Number 4

Secrecy at all cost

Number 5

Say it as **explained to you** and not as you **actually**

Felt it

Number 6

you have only one person that you can give and receive love from

and that's **Ms. Polly**

Number 7

Never ask for something you need

You don't deserve it

Number 8

BEG---------------------------------at all cost for love

Number 9

take all responsibility

Number 10

never express pain

Number 11

go to church and read the Bible

--------------------**nothing happened**

number 12

accept all

Confessions

People always encourage you to tell your story

but

when I think about my story

I never really know where to begin

 "Which part of my story would you like me to tell you first? "

My butterflies would thrash

And my stomach would lurch

I knew a punch Or hit would likely meet me when I got home

I cried myself to sleep every night, my nerves were shot

I cried and cried

everywhere I turned, people told me to

Pray it away

I thought

End

My life

It seemed more freeing

death Seemed more freeing

Unless you've been punched, slapped, talked about, slapped, kicked in the face, shoved against the wall, you will never understand that depth of pain

The death

The death of innocence that enters your body at such a young age

'cause I gotta be

In DM U

Dorm mat University

I Need A Life Jacket

Can anyone see I am dying inside?

I'm dying to be seen

I have pasted my story against this black wall

in my box

I thought my being was defined by everyone outside

I was present but absent

I was physically there

I was inwardly gone

that's why it was so easy to take that extra step

to plan my terminal end

a steak Knife

after dinner

I would slit my wrists and let the rest of my existence evaporate

The mist of evaporation after a heavy rainfall

I just couldn't take it anymore

I did not want to hear any more; self-conscious of my blackness,

my big lips and the scars on my back to remind me

Never Enough

Although we were watching news about Crimes

My terrorism was within

My existence numbed every day

A slit to the wrist would end this never-ending hell!

I carried the weight of fear in my loins

Anger pangs

I'm sorry if you don't understand this glaze

I'm sorry that you have no room for this pain

I've been praying

I've been calling

but where is this God?

Where is the savior who said he was my rod?

I'm looking for a shoulder to lay my head on, but someone has mentioned

that this is all wrong

 I'm told that these moments are all gone

What kind of God is he?

Let me experience this stress

In Church,

Patent leather shoes and Fanning hands that surround me

Amazed at how silent everyone is when my secret is so profound

Can these people see me over their hymn books?

-----------------cuz I've been questioning the spirit

I hear screams and crawls

in all of this commotion

my soul is still empty

This path

'This path is usually narrow, and I have been standing'

I remember the valley and the tapered path that provided the pebble

Stones gripped my ability to walk

This path appeared to be dumb

Matter of fact

I was laughed at on this path

Beat on this path

clobbered on this path

lied to on this path

but I still remember standing

This path was a reminder of something new

Slanted, I sided with the skew

the logic of this path

Money cannot buy this path

Prejudice cannot thwart this path

This path is my path

the sensory mechanisms cannot be derailed on the outside

I shortened my path for your understanding on the inside

I was just beginning this path

It allowed humans to storm out this ------path

It has been the same in every season

this path has claimed my heart

isn't it funny that people have so many questions about this path?

Tell me your deepest secret about this path

why won't you share your worst moment on this path?

This path is genuine

this path is the Cornerstone of my soul

This path cannot be tried on without authenticity

The tears

the sweat

the blood

This path is one that few dare to walk

That is why I want to know

-----------are you walking on yours?

Solace

I wish I never had to write this poem, but my bruises are so visible I must explain

Staring at my reflection, reminding me I was not acceptable

She said I would never be accepted

I did not pass the paper bag test and so I could not be beautiful

I prostituted my soul and hoped for a grandmother of stone

This stone is still more precious than the mud of my existence

In tears

I learned the backstroke and remembered the knife of those words

there was spit in my face

a pot cover to the head

There was a screaming rage

-9My stomach turned every time I heard her scream

It was like a prize call from Ed McMahon, and I glided in my imagination into an igloo

there, I recognized my altitude

Unfortunately, I also saw the real you

and I knew my soul was saved

Reflections

I Ponder

My new story is about to begin

every time I enter the day

a piece of yesterday grips my heart

---- I continue to look into the mirror that is Straight Ahead

unfortunately, that **vagrant** is behind my right shoulder

reminding me of the picture they painted of me

to remember

I take **my invisible marker and remove them like I would white-out**

a misspelled word

I stand and look at the mirror again to see evasive blooms

These blooms are breath-taking

They remind me of my promise

The scent is reminiscent of new grass

the leaves have a fluorescent Hue and remind me of my Foundation,

which cannot be seen

but is so intensely felt

in a moment of majesty

I can see my **Eagle Soul**

Here where I allow my Chronicles out of my box

Face to Face

No happy birthdays for me

no happy birthdays for me

No happy birthdays for Sidonia

no happy birthdays for you

This **box** I am in

I love this **box**

I look out through my window and you look into mine

 it's very lonely here and

I don't mind it

I actually have learned to live in this place of loneliness

A place where I don't have to defend my truth

this place where I don't have to appease you

I did not cause this

I was just

four

I was four

I was ten

 I was 13

I was 16

 I was 22

Yeah

those were my years

Beauty was never allowed

I was to be, simply be,

Invisible

I learned to take away any feeling

to take away any sensation

any desire

any hope

I learned it well

I always had a glimmer of hope that you would face yourself

Now

I ACCEPT YOUR DENIAL

I'm still a person

I'm still a person

I cried

cried and

cried and

I stared at myself in the mirror for 15 minutes daily

I got used to staring at myself in the mirror because

I always wanted to know I was alive

So you want to know what it's like to "act" happy after being punched in the face?

It's like dressing up for Halloween

When it really is not Halloween

It is **every single day**

Like dressing up for your favorite play, right before your lead role,

Only to be told you were just a stand in

Like staring at someone who's frowning at you because they don't know you're watching

And they look off stage and see that an audience is viewing

You're smiling because the cameras are on

Your stomach drops and you are at your lowest point

You reside to nothingness

you actually welcome it

YOU realize **no one will fight for you** because **no one is there**

You don't know how to reach out

you don't know who to trust

you don't know who to laugh with

you don't know when to be angry

when not to be angry

when to have pity

when not to have pity

you don't know if someone is showing concern or if they're pitying you

you don't know if they're manipulating you or

-------------------------------------if they're using you to feel better about themselves

Damn

At that lowest point when you don't feel s***

you need to drink something, touch something

point to something

Just to feel

Sidonia: 120 Days Choreopoem

What would you do with 120 days?

You've been trying to see things through

What would you do with 120 days?

See, the life I had before was full of uncertainty

Clogged, like puss formed in a broken hair follicle

Vague, like a blurry vision of Michelangelo's greatest work

Crushed, like a smoothie without syrup

Broken, like a piece of shattered glass on a carpet

Squeamish, like a snake slithering through

My Past, Present, Future

Contained, like cookies in a cookie jar

Hidden, inside of a cabinet

away from reach

Sloppy, like ketchup on a white shirt

Hidden, like a black marker

On a black portrait, on a black wall, in a black hole

Forgotten, like gristle on a steak

Useless, like a baby diaper

Tired, like the eyes of a ninety-six-year old

Like the jacket of a drowned victim

Silenced, like a muzzled lion

In the back, under the table

Unconfrontational

overly apologetic

Like a crack addict, addicted to a behavior that is

addicted to the pain inflicted

By an Inflicted person whose infliction was infected with integrated images from prior individual incantations of pain, covered in fits of outward manifestation

Projected onto this being

Stuck, like butter on a cheese croissant

Moving one foot forward while the other is left in 1982

Inch by inch

Row by row, but no current in my river to float

In the middle of the titanic

With no score for my movie

Shattered by what could have been

Grieving all that was lost

Looking at life through a kaleidoscope

of

Fear, resentment and misperception

Holding this voice back in silence

To respect lies

Letting lies outweigh truth

Respecting lies

Consuming lies

Hiding my truth to respect the family of fear

But this consistent wandering has allowed me to hit a Boulder

A boulder has been hit

A boulder that would forever shake my world

It is the Big in my Big Bang Theory

It cracked open truth I would have never imagined

It sent a beam of fire in my inmost being and cracked through the pain

Of a mask that looked like success to the world

It said

I KNOW YOUR EXPERIENCE, I KNOW YOUR STORY, I KNOW YOUR PAIN, I SAW YOUR TEARS, I KNOW WHEN YOU WANTED TO END IT, I KNOW THE ABANDONMENT, I KNOW THE ISOLATION, I KNOW THE LOSS, I KNOW THE STORY, I KNOW THE HARDSHIP, I KNOW THE LOSS YEARS, I KNOW THE POOR CHOICES, I KNOW A LIFE OF PAIN

I ALSO KNOW

IT AIN'T OVER

IT AIN'T OVER

CAN YOU LIVE DRASTICALLY DIFFERENT?

WHAT WOULD HAPPEN IF YOU HAD 120 DAYS TO BEGIN A DRASTICALLY DIFFERENT LIFE?

WHAT WOULD HAPPEN IF YOU CUT OLD TIES?

WHAT WOULD HAPPEN IF YOU DID SOMETHING THIS YEAR AND SURPRISED YOURSELF?

WHAT WOULD HAPPEN IF YOUR YES WAS YES AND NO WAS NO?

WHAT WOULD HAPPEN IF YOU LET TRUTH REIGN?

WHAT WOULD HAPPEN IF YOU FORGAVE LIFE'S HARDSHIPS?

WHAT WOULD HAPPEN IF YOU RECEIVED REDEMPTION FOR ALL THE YEARS Lost?

WHAT WOULD HAPPEN IF YOU ONLY HAD 120 DAYS?

You are beautiful

No matter what anyone says

I hear your cry

I hear your sigh

I know you want to be ok

And nothing can hold you back from meeting destiny

Nothing can hold you down

I hear your cry

I hear your sigh

I hear all the naysayers have been pickin' on you

This is your time

To own your life

This is your time

Your season to be strong

I hear your cry

I hear your sigh

This is the moment to live your destiny

You are all that you need

To make your life better

You are all that you need

To make your life strong

Repeat

You are beautiful

Dedicated to that little girl

The Fourth Wind

See the winds

Captivate my breath and circle around three times plus one

Looking for a corner to grasp the past

The winds remind me

Transition is underlying

And The first wind is knocked down

I was a vagrant collecting heart food from the wrong store

Yeah, that first wind, it knocked me down and told me not to think of getting

down, So I assumed the position

My hands formed fists, ready to punch any enemy--

Even the ones I hadn't met

Numbing my existence

Knocking out my spirit

Sealing the lips that told me to trust

The Second wind rolled me over and I blinked

I thought love had opened a new seed

Not realizing my wounds would still bleed

Causing me to mistake attention for love

I longed for laughter living without loss

Arms holding me would still pay too much of a cost

And see, the third wind simultaneously fused the first and second wind saying

I know you ain't here trying again

Stop

Look at you

I knocked you with these winds

Stop trying

Look at the Judas's

Look at the Jezebels

Look at the world, it is hopeless

Why try

Why not settle

When will you stop this faith thing and tap into reality?

When are you going to adjust your philosophy so you can live only for today?

Drink a little something, feel a little something

No one cares about this too-deep-to-sleep chaos you are bringing

Rephrase (You Are Beautiful…Harmony)

This message has been interrupted, in a moment you will hear a beep for thirty seconds

Beep

Beep Beep

There is no one more faithful

Faithful to feel the flaws of failure and fear

Forcing fleers of flames from lies felt early

I can observe this fourth wind because it consumes me

It's the filling in my cavity, bridge over waters

The Ring in my binder

The Back to my earring

The Saran for my wrap

The tic and tac

The Cover to my pot

The Glue to my transparence

Fourth wind is

Fourth wind has

I think I have been swept

This is my day

This is my hour

This is my Day

This is my hour

This is my time

This is my time

This is my day

This is my time

I am standing on the shore of time

Oceans

Asking you for the call

But the tide comes to the edge

I wonder if the water

Will touch my feet?

Am I too far for the algae to brush against my heels?

I have been watching for the sun

Watching for the sun to set in the east and to set in the west

And to set in the North and to set in the south

My head down, I thought the waves forgot about me

And then the water flushed over my ankles and I laughed and fell on my day

Realizing this was day!

My Uncle Turtle

Invisible was my self-definition.

One thing I did love about being raised by my Ms. Polly is that I did have an Uncle called Turtle.

I loved Uncle Turtle.

He was a man that loved to dress up on Sunday mornings.

On certain Sundays I would be forced to wake up early to hear my Uncle Turtle preach to a Pentecostal Christian Church. I

loved watching his performance.

Uncle Turtle would wear the same red shiny shoes when it was his day to preach. On preach days, Uncle Turtle would slick down his fresh perm and finish off his white starch suit with shiny red shoes

He made sure to have a starch white suit on and a fresh perm, to slick his hair down for the day of his presentation.

He loved to talk about the role of faith and how we all had to pray daily for God to give us strength.

'Honestly, Uncle Turtle looked like James Brown when he was driving home a key point in the sermon.'

He got us all so excited

There would be one or two people doing cartwheels as the pianist raised the level of renditions on the keys.

We sang spirituals and felt like we were on fire by the time the service ended. Everyone loved Uncle Turtle.

My thought of Uncle Turtle changed when I observed a peculiar trait about him.

After church service we all returned home for a major dinner.

Ms. Polly took me and placed me in the tub.

 At six years old I was frozen with fear.

I was her robot. My caretaker scared me so much I would flinch and raise my hands to protect my face if she decided it was my day to get

beat. I did this once and fell down two flights of stairs. Child protection service came to the rescue but I was too scared to tell them the truth.

I zoned out and played cartoons as Ms. Polly ranted to Uncle Turtle as to how I was a curse.

Uncle Turtle would see me standing there with the "HELP ME" look but would look away every time **our eyes met.**

 How could my superhero witness this treatment and not step in? As God's representative, I felt that his hesitance to step in was my just **punishment.**

Uncle Turtle was my first realization that **god could not be real.**

Uncle Turtle **turned his head**

 I sat at the table with scars on my back, arms and chest.

Uncle Turtle told us all to bow and pray before we ate.

All I could do was bow and cry. I

ate my meal one morsel at a time, hoping for nightfall to come.

Ms. Polly redemption

A rare talk with Ms. Polly

forty years later and the knots in my stomach still turn

I stare at Ms. Polly to understand her footprints

at another time Ms. Polly was a Baby

full of innocence and promise

When did this villain within her arrive?

What made her turn colder than ice?

Who quenched her desire to learn, grow and explore?

'Ms. Polly came with one tear in her eye

My neighbors told me she stayed at the Days Inn across the street for four

days, waiting to see my BMW pull up into the driveway

It was late when I started up the stairs with my carry-on,

and there, standing at the door, was MS. POLLY.'

She had a way of holding door handles and I knew that it was

 MS. POLLY

 my hands balled up into a fist.

My life flashed before me as I thought of her words,

her stares remind me that I was NOTHING

My inner child said…It is OKAY

I took a breath

Ms. Polly interrupted

"I will not be really long

I understand if you never speak to me again.

My days were so blue, I forgot what it was like to conversate in the light.

I always wanted the love of my family, but I was also given up for adoption.

Seeing you, made me angry;

Your innocence

Your easy laugh

Your chocolate skin

PISSED ME OFF

You reminded me of myself in so many ways

But yet….

No matter what I said to kick you to the floor, you still kept your dignity.

What made you so different to me?

Truly, I have been BESIDE myself;

I sleep in a tiny room now

Uncle Turtle has moved on.

The house is quite empty

I often see how badly I treated you and hate myself for it

I feel like a USED rag."

MY REPLY

Started with a dry eye

I shed so many tears, there were not more to lose

I saw raisin hands and I knew for sure that those devilish words would not grip me anymore

I took a deep sigh and invited her inside

I made her favorite chocolate and heated up a frozen chicken pot pie

I sat it on the table and then began to stare

How do I begin, what do I say?

and at this point,

Do I even care?

We think Children Forget their early years

Until they turn 40 and...

evening dreams make them sweat

They Begin to REMEMBER

Little SIDONIA Still remembers...But She realizes she is all grown UP

I continued to stare for five minutes or more

Until I saw Ms. Polly lose her grip on the door

I said,

"Oh no, please come back and share your piece

I am grown now and want you to be able to release

All that has been in you, that has imploded you for sure

I am not that timid girl who was so innocent and pure

I can at least give you a few moments to talk

And then we can see if it will be our time to walk."

She looked down at her feet and started to cry

I tried to see her, but there was too much water in her eyes

She said, I truly did not know the pain that I caused

The more I hit you, my mind confronted my past with every pause

I never thought it was all that bad

Until I would see how easy it was for me to be glad

After moments of pounding your back in the floor

Closing the windows so no one could see your sores

But look at you today, you always kept that fighter within

No matter what I said to you

you would never allow me to bend

Or break your spirit cuz you always dreamed big

And now today you are changing lives

And I only first saw you as a twig."

Well thanks Ms. Polly for the pain I had to see

It taught me to forgive my past in order to be free

I know we may never understand all of you

But please go find your garden; there is still time to BLOOM.

A NEW MANTRA

Forty has a way of telling your truth in a way you did not ask for

What does the SCALE say?

Who was that person I met at the last meeting?

How long has it been since X has passed?

A time to say all the hours of tomorrow are not promised, so where does this leave me today?

open the doors to new possibilities

'It feels like I'm at a green traffic light, expecting it to turn red'

I put my head down to turn on GPS

GPS

Where is the definition of SUCCESS?

Was I supposed to have reached it?

Exactly what is this mountain supposed to feel like?

#Stayhome

My third glass of VODKA and my memories are here

Nothing else to do but try to get clear

Looking at the images that were never there

Worried about iReports, but no knowledge of how you are in despair

That last conversation was not the end

My conscious told me to sit on this bench

Mask is on and I still worry

That our talk was meaningless, and it caused us to leave each other in a hurry

But---it's Quarantine time---so when will you come clean

And say I am so sorry for always being so MEAN?

I have accomplished a lot and have the stories of three lives

But nothing can ever take the place of having my tribe

I have now accepted your Denial is at stake

I have come **out of my box and can no longer be fake**

I have spoken to counsel and prayed 1 million times

But I got to a place where my drug was my grind

Now I know that this situation is not really about you

It's about your hidden pain that all started when you were two

I am so sorry for your loss

That pain that caused you to bully, in order to feel like a Boss

I am sad that no one likes to ring your bell

Or that there is no internal water in your well

I have finally released those hidden pains

Now I am ready to receive the Abundance of Rain

I had to release you in order to be free

Accept your behavior and maltreatment since the age of three

It is now okay to never bring it up again

I have left that old zip code

Empty Trees

Stop looking at empty trees

You keep walking down a dead-end trail

Always dreaming when the layout confirms there is no passage

It is not because the ground is not there to dig the path.

There are people who have the shovel, but they are too scared to pick it up.

They also want to pretend that a path is there, knowing they have planted bob wire behind the bush.

Yet you keep dreaming of a time when there was a trail that led to laughter

Over the years, rose thorns have covered the patch and poison ivy has infiltrated that passage

Aren't your legs itching?

You really wish that passage was there

You cried for it

Lost your identity for it

Lost your appetite for it

Hoping for something the shovel-holders would deem a priority

So, in protest, you

Neglect your feet

Instead of turning 360

You stand sideways

Hoping someone would grab that shovel. Not realizing in the same breath

That a new path, with marble, has been elevated for you

There are golden columns that lead to a personalized jacuzzi, named

Dreams

Leaving

I cry for the old passage

I cry for your ignorance

I cry for your inability to let go

I cry for your bruised elbows

I wish you could move past shame.

I wish you could embrace me in this passage

I wish you would stand and help me

But.......

I am ready to make room to Reignite all that was lost.

This box no longer serves me.

This box is no longer safe. It has become a toxic box of Shame that I am ready to step out of.

I am ready to Upgrade my life with no apology

Ready to soar on this new path. New hearts. New moments. New horizons.

Sunset

Fly Like An Eagle

You're never too old to reach a new destination

Time and longevity have made you scared

Remember, I hold your hand in all seasons

You have to be convinced

Not of what others say

You need to be convinced that I can renew you

I can uphold you

I can heal you

I can open new doors for you

I can make a way of escape

I can show you what to take and what not to take

I can be the one to tell you Yes or No!

If only one person

Would just believe

Would just open their heart

Would clear their motivation

Would lend an ear

Would lend a hand

Would loosen their fists

I would be able to come in and do my job

You are your strength

Don't let your fire trials rob you of victories

Remember

I will hold your hand

I am firm like a tree

I am sprouting like a flower

I sing like a bird

I dance like a giraffe

I am the ROCK

I AM the one who can redeem you

Lend your ear

Lend your time

Lend your energy

Fight through depression

Fight through heartache

Fight through low self-esteem

Fight through Anger

Come to Peace

Peace is the answer

The only way to calm

The only way out of fear

Deliverance is found

Dreams are answered and hearts

Are renewed.

Unveiling ME

It Is ME TIME and I am ready for something new

I'm ready to come out because I have waited for 35 years for this vision of a new me to come to be

Everything that I was born to be, fully allowed

Leaving old stains that no longer stay stuck on my shirt

Ready to love me, ready to start over, ready for something new, because everything I was told came from someone else's third eye. Everything I was told came from someone who had a cracked mirror and, now that I'm standing in front of a full mirror, able to see my true reflection, I wonder if I was looking at the right person.

Today, I make a vow to better my life

Today, I make a vow to be a responsible individual who

Speaks

Up

For myself

Today, I have stopped apologizing for what you could never resolve

Today, I am ready to close the chapter

Today, I am ready to close all the chapters that reminded me that I was worth ---- less

It is absolutely funny to think that we are in a time of isolation

Because I'm only 37 yet I have been isolated in my mind for 50 years

I guess we can all relate; that we understand what it means to be insulated

Wanting to speak

Wanting to come out

Wanting something more

But scared of what is on the other side of that door

With hands clasped

Waiting

Waiting

Waiting

Waiting

Waiting

Waiting for something else

Wishing you were someone else

Wishing I was someone else

Hating the Vine

And as much as I hate the Vine, I recognize the blooms, and as much as I hate the blooms, I recognize that I share a bloom on this Vine

Waiting

Waiting

Waiting

Until I finally had the gumption to picture myself on this boat in the middle of an ocean. An ocean deep and wide enough to show me my limited viewpoint

Now, I can set sail and see my reflection against the River

Now, I can see you in the wind and wish you the best

I can have a silent funeral that I will always remember

Acknowledging the things that I will never be able to control

But allowing the breeze to graze my arm reminds me that there is more in store

In this moment, I can finally have my peace

So, today I make an appointment with peace

I'm determined to let him guide me

There are relationships I must end

For peace and I to grow

Any giant distracting me from peace must be released

Peace is my only destiny

The ultimate home for peace and me in the ground

I'm not afraid of our home

Whoops, I must go

I don't want to be late for our appointment Dan's hot

Empowerment

With open eyes, your mountain is there, you stand erect and look to the stars' glare

Remember, the light within yearns to expand

Set your foot firmly

Commit to a plan

Nothing to lose

You are on Your way

Boldly move forward

And dream today

Uncle turtle Part 2

I went to uncle turtle's house because he begged me to come over

He wanted to explain why he had not stepped in

Why he Could not lift his head for the duration of his life

He looked me in the face and sincerely said:

"Sidonia, I know you're a grown woman now and there are so many questions that I have failed to answer.

There's no way that I could actually take the 40 years and tell you how my life impacted yours."

He began to tell me:

"I had to move out of the house; I would have loved to stay if it were healthy. I always wanted to know why I couldn't remember being tucked into bed at night.

Why couldn't I remember a time when I was affirmed?

No Daddy

No Mother

No one

I was Angry

I turned inwards

That is why I always look checked out

Why I always slept

Forgive me

It seems I just don't know what to say

For me, it is better to stay inside silent rooms and clear my mind

But so much of my life has passed me by

Although I saw miss Polly treat you so poorly

She was a friend to me

In my time, people said you were loved if you were fed

And that's what we tried to do with you

You know I wasn't given a fair deal in my time; we had limited resources

In my time we did not have all of the opportunities that you have today

But if you don't find a way to deal with your anger,

It will bleed into all of the empty spaces of your life

My response:

Uncle turtle

Do you know how many years I spent questioning my identity?

My face looking down at all times

Always feeling broken

I always vowed that one day I would have my own child

I pictured what it would be like to hold that special being in my mind

I held her close and could see her two Afro puffs with bubbles

She was smiling and she walked with me

Through her life

3 to 9

We quantum leaped to a birthday party

All the candles lit her chocolate face in excitement

She could not wait to blow out the candles

She quantum leaped

She rested her little head on my chest

Stories of Courage

It takes Courage to leave the Familiar

I was 16

Walking down the street

I was walking in the city

Past broken beer bottles

Past cats calling me for attention

Walking past the booming systems and, at times, Yellow Caution Tape

To avoid the urban tragedies before me

I dreamed of BECOMING

I saw new glimpses at 19, as I learned about this Idea of Self-Acceptance

And I Dreamed of BECOMING

All that was not expected of me

A good day is when we would go outside and let the water from the hydrants splash all over our bodies. 'Tito Puente's could be heard playing out of Abuelas home, reminding us that it was time to come home before the lights turned on. We all knew that an urban lower middle-class existence meant hard work, avoiding peer pressure and getting to the other side of this "AMERICAN DREAM."

I worked in Television, I wrote for the paper, I spoke on the radio, and I wrote in journals from

1995---to 2005---2015 and I wondered What BECOMING would feel like

I wanted to BECOME someone who accepted myself

I wanted to BECOME confident in a manner that surpassed my internal flaws

I wanted to BECOME Five-Star and believe that my Dreams of Turning On the Lights in my life and those of others could be tangible

And as I dreamed, I just Began

2008—Hey Ladies want to come over for an empowerment circle

I saw 4

2010

I saw 12

I took a PAUSE

And Procrastination became my Twin Sister

My poems-----In a Box called Will Get To It

My Goal of motivational speaking, books and training...All in a box called ONE DAY

My Brother-Familiarity

 would show up everyday with calls that said, "Wow! You're doing so much Allana!)

But in my heart I knew I could do more. If I would just be honest with SELF, I could say NO
 to things that sounded good and begin to get clear around my
Distant Cousin POTENTIAL
A solid Incubation----would remind me to look at the little nine-year old girl and determine that there was some inner healing that had to occur for the 40-year-old BEST version of ALLANA to SHOW UP.

And I heard
"Allana, if you are to be this business woman, you have to believe you are beautiful and valuable and nothing about you Is a mistake!
Can you say it with me: I am beautiful, I am valuable, and nothing about me is a mistake.

What if I told you
        everything could change in two days

Take off everything for a few moments
 Step into the **HOT BOX**
Imaginary Hat of the Past (Throw it to the Floor)
Hand on the hat that has defined you for the past and present success and failures
Put it to the floor

Take in a deep breath

Step into this new space

Your New SPACE

Music Interlude_____

Take Space

123 Take Space

123 Take Space

Looking mighty fine

Looking mighty fine

YES-------Was not easy

*This **Journey of courage***

I began

I took out my phone

Got on IG with Zero viewers

Hello to none

And No one was there

No one was there

And with time, things began to change

See----I want to tell you about the Bamboo tree

It is a significant plant

Takes five years to show

When I heard Les Brown mention the Bamboo

I had to research the Bamboo tree

This tree must be watered for a five-year period

In this time nothing happening

In this time, farmer is waiting

I don't know if you have been waiting for your **BAMBOO**

Dream *to show up*

Waiting for 3-5 years waiting for this new dream to begin

Why don't you Stand Up if you are excited

Stand up

If you are ready to say I am ready to

UPGRADE MY LIFE

www.ingramcontent.com/pod-product-compliance
Lightning Source LLC
Chambersburg PA
CBHW040325220526
45473CB00009B/2574